LOPSIDED HALO

Lopsided Halo

by
WILLIAM M. BARRETT

POETS OF AMERICA PUBLISHING
COMPANY
New York, N. Y.

Copyright, 1960, by
POETS OF AMERICA PUBLISHING
COMPANY

All Rights Reserved

Printed in United States of America

DEDICATION

To my wife:
For whom poetry is music
And music, undoubtedly, poetry.

ACKNOWLEDGMENTS

American Weave, Anthropos, Contemporary Ohio Poetry, International Poetry Review, OPS Bulletin, Ohio Poetry Review, Wisconsin Poetry Journal, Poets of America Anthology 1958 and Vespers.

CONTENTS

Lopsided Halo	1
Intimacy	2
Turmoil	2
Suppose	3
The Wanderer	4-7
Think of the Wild Geese Flying	8
To This I Cling	9
Morning Stroll	10
Interim	11-12
Nature	13
And the Walls	14
Why	15
The Age of Innocence	16
Outward Bound	17
For To-morrow	18
To-morrow Too	19
Impassionata	20
Miami Holiday	21-22
Perspective	22
Where the Willows Wander in the Wind	23
Parable of the Seven Fishes	24
Still Waters	25
The Parasite	26
Forever the Wishing Well	27-28
Fear	29

CONTENTS

Mississippi	30
Next Stop Scottsboro	31
The Torch Burns Low	32
Charity	33
Bleary Needs a Lawyer	34
Schizo—The Poet	35
Driftwood—Thirty Three	36-37
Song and Laughter	37
Carrousel	38
The Forgotten Man	39
Trail's End	40
Sunset Through a Periscope	41
On Parade	42
A Posthumous Award	43
Ashes on Okinawa	44-45
Italy	46
Red Wine Returning	47
Wind of the East	48
The Merry-Go-Round Stands Still	49
I Have a Comfortable God	50
Observed by a Celestial Visitor	51
Valhalla and the Angels	52-53
Sunday in Heaven	53
Kinderspiel	54-55
How Is It?	56
Candleglow	57
Going Down	58
Never the Loon	59

PREFACE

Too often in reading a volume of contemporary poetry, one is disappointed on finding that it consists almost entirely of clever exercises in technique, on subjects devoid of intellectual or emotional impact. While it is true that the subject alone does not make the poem, and that an inferior poet will produce a bad work no matter how significant the theme, this is not a valid reason why technically competent poets should avoid weighty subjects and focus, instead, upon tiny fragments of experience, creating word-puzzles of precious nothingness. To the reader surfeited with the poetry of calculated whimpering, William Barrett's LOPSIDED HALO is an exciting departure from the usual. Here is poetry of depth and scope. While some of the selections are personal in theme and mood, others have a sociological, historical, or mythological background. Mr. Barrett knows that the private world is not the only world worth writing about. The element of universality, too often missing in modern poetry, is dynamically present in his book.

For this reader, one of the striking facets of Mr. Barrett's style is his ability to explore and illuminate a subject from several points of view. He is a poet of multiple perspectives. There is something in his work that is best described as "dramatic empathy," the ability to enter into the consciousness of others and to articulate the throb of their lives. Every one of us is an island; but some can reach into the solitude of another, share with that other a vision of the world, and know that no man is utterly alone. It is the gift of empathy, and Mr. Barrett has it in abundance.

Aware of the complexity of any totally-realized event, Mr. Barrett does not attempt to simplify a problem in terms of black and white, absolute good and absolute evil. He is under no inner compulsion to prove that one position has a monopoly on truth and all other positions are in error. In "I Have a Comfortable

God," the poet enters into the mind of a Mexican peasant for whom God is in His heaven, but all is *not* well with the world. "Valhalla and the Angels" is a brilliantly imaginative treatment of the conflict between Christianity and the religion of the Norsemen—a whimsical poem with serious overtones. "Observed by a Celestial Visitor," written from the vantage point of a Martian or a Venusian, puts us earth-dwellers to shame for the mess we have made of our planet. "Ashes on Okinawa" is written from the point of view of a Japanese soldier toward the end of World War II. In this poem, Mr. Barrett's power of empathetic identification is most vividly illustrated. Here is a poet who has no ideological axe to grind. His ability to see a situation from divergent angles is a rare phenomenon, and one that is sorely needed to counteract the mental fascism of dogmatists in politics and religion who have embraced the most pernicious error of which the human mind is capable, namely, the belief that a person or organization holds the eternal and universal truth, and that all opposing positions should be suppressed.

A predilection for large themes and the gift of dramatic empathy are among William Barrett's outstanding characteristics; but these attributes, however commendable, would not suffice in themselves to entitle him to the name of poet, were his work deficient in the original metaphors and burning phrases that are the essence of poetry. Throughout his book he demonstrates that one can write communicative poetry on important subjects without sacrificing the gains of modern poetry since the advent of the Symbolists and the Imagists. As in all distinctively modern poetry, we find figures with several strata of meaning, and rhythms determined by mood and emotion rather than by purely mechanical considerations. We find, also, a complete freedom in choice of subject matter.

Mr. Barrett is a poet because his phrases have richness and compression that distinguish poetry from prose. He writes of "fear-freighted ghosts" roaming through the "unswept alleys of the mind," and of "mute, unwrapped mummies,/Skeletons of old lies." In "posthumous Award" he speaks of those "Who worship silently/The unheard god of brotherhood." In "Kinderspiel" he writes of "the slide-rule heavens/The sun's unfailing time-table."

He can look at a stream and see it "tiptoeing from here into eternity." In "Miami Holiday," the poet, in a moment of mystical identification with all the generations of the past, present, and future, realizes that "a billion atoms before me/And a billion atoms after/Will seek to finger this merchandise of stars." Writing of World War II in "Red Wine Returning," he gives us memorable phrases like, "That year the devil was a bartender,/Red wine flowed into filthy gutters." In "How Is It," he celebrates the wonder and curiosity of a child with the desire "to wander in and out among the stars/And tie a string between his heaven and earth/And bring them to his fingertips." Like all real poets, William Barrett is a maker of phrases that the reader cannot forget.

ALFRED DORN
January 1, 1960

LOPSIDED HALO

The hero rode on his rented horse
In a blazing path that marked his course,
The multitude in faceless mass
Proclaimed the honor of his class.

The hero rode,
But his spirit flew
Beyond the horse and the avenue.

The hero rode,
But his thoughts were sparse
And chided him for the futile farce.

The hero rode,
But his army lay
Beyond the seas in deep decay.

The hero rode,
But he heard no shout
From the dead men riding all about.

INTIMACY
(for Eleanore)

How microscopic are the thoughts
Momentarily lighting my lamp with stabbing beams
Into the far corners of my consciousness.
Instantly
I see you finely etched in silhouette:
And the many hues and garments which I clothed you in,
Dissolved.

Come sight and ripened knowledge,
Vision at my finger tips:
And then I know—
This swift embracing recognition,
This intimacy and understanding,
Is love.

TURMOIL

Blue waters racing with dark clouds
And an unseen wind howling
As they fight it out in an empty ring
On a heaving, bleak and empty ocean.

Blue sky and a zephyr blowing
And the listening heather humming to tune:
A startled woodbird leaving its nesting
Roused by a sudden unseen fear.

Blue moods and an earthless yearning—
Vague thoughts which no words describe
Sired by the winds and waters turning
The dark tempestuous loam, the mind.

SUPPOSE

Suppose
The sky was so round and blue
And the air was soft, and wind you knew
Was pointing down where the swallows flew
And tugged at your shirt and scolded you.

Suppose
You dreamed of a day to come
When the chores of the world were finished and done
And your fingers beat to the rhythm of fun
And tangoed a tune where your cares had gone.

Suppose
You heard—and your ears caught fire
And your eyes looked out and you saw the mire,
The grubby world and the souls for hire—
And you chucked it all for an ivory spire.

Suppose
You dwelt in a land of dreams
And only saw what you thought it seems
While floating by on shadowy beams
In a shoreless world of endless streams.

Suppose
You woke from a dream so bright
And looked around for a gleam of light
And found the world full of weeds and blight
And headed for shore to set it right.

THE WANDERER

The memory of a child is blurred and lost
As a thousand fleeting pictures hover
And vaguely stir the crusting layers.
But some, where fertile seeds are deeply sown,
Find sudden flowering as old thoughts return
And flash remembrance through the mist-filled years.

I see again the swelling ocean foam
And toss upon its heaving crest
An ugly beetle of an iron ship,
While I within it, gay and much too young
To fear the sullen, bulging white-capped hills,
Nor the deepening chasms which followed soon.
The rising spray seemed friendly though it wet
And chilled, it made me shrill for the pure joy,
(As children will.)

But that delight soon passed.
I now remember ancient tenements,
(Manhattan's shame) and they became my home.
I went to crowded schools, but soon grew up
A bright-eyed boy, who bent on seeing things,
Grew sad and pensive at its sordidness:
Who poured his eager heart and youthful mind
To bring more light where so much darkness grew:
Who grew rebellious with the passing years,
And bitter when the world unheeding passed:
Who found a city filled with motley creeds,
With strange and tangled backgrounds and beliefs,
Where Jew and Christian, Russian, Swede and Pole
Were herded into Ghettos, penned in flats,
Driven into sweat-shops and to mills
To make the grist of new and more appalling hells
Than even Europe could be proud of.

Small wonder that the simple peasant grew
To lush and sickening ripeness overnight.

From tiller of the soil or artisan,
With one swift stroke, a cog he had become,
A robot geared to moving parts and wheels
Which droned and clashed through endless dismal hours,
Until eternity was real and round
And made of monstrous fly-wheels geared to hell,
And turning, turning, grinding human souls
Bound and lashed to evil, grinning circles,
Growing larger, ever larger, melting
From the finite, into the infinite.

The vision of my days at school returns.
(The boy was still a boy, and yet, not quite.)
The ancient worlds came tumbling out of books
And blossomed forth before my eager eyes.
Dim tribes scattered over Asia's plains
Spread westward into Europe, founded Greece,
And built a shining temple to the mind
So pure, that later ages sought in vain
To find the root or reason for the flower.
It lived and breathed its glory all too soon,
And slept full many ages ere it rose
From the buried ashes that was Greece
To find once more a world where reason dwelt,
Wherein the forum once again was king,
And Aristotle crowned as Reason's Prince.

Some happy tribes strayed southward to the Nile
And found Judea as a favored land.
They brought the Spirit and the Law to man.
Their key to life was justice, man with man,
And over all, one God omnipotent.
Too soon the yielding fruit was scattered wide
By angry, brutal, jealous clods of men,
But as each seed fell into foreign soil,
There gardens grew, and when the time was ripe,
The world partook of feasts Israel prepared.

In quick succession mighty Rome stepped forth.
From sullen fledgling suckling at the teats
Of an old mother wolf, it raised a brood
Of wolf-like men who came and conquered all
The ancient worlds their greedy eyes espied:
Who proved that force engendered still more force,
It had its futile hour and then passed on,
A victim of its own brutality.
And time which had extinguished in their hearts
The thoughts and lust for conquest and for power,
And had implanted music, art and love,
Stood still, nay—trod backwards, back to Rome,
To Caesars flailing legions, bringing death
To friend and foe alike. Death to Rome,
To Romans, death to music, science, art.
Unhappy Caesars sleeping through the age
While puppy Duces swaggered over Rome
And dreamed to be its master's masterpiece.

So many things a boy could learn at school
If he but have the mind to pluck the fruits
Or drink in sparkling, never drying streams:
So many cloistered pearls are strewn about
In every nook and corner of the world,
I marvel now how little of its wealth
I thought to take, and yet what joy I found
In such few treasures as were showered on me.
It seemed the world must grow by leaps and bounds,
Each son a giant, towering his sire,
Climbing up with sure and steady feet,
Until the vales of yesterday were small
And puny things to sweat and fret about.
For upward, yonder, lies a tableland,
Above the clouds, clear, dry and rich,
And surely youth could reach it ere the sun
Would cast its final shadows on the hills.

What futile dreams an aging man can have.
The past seems thin and silly, like a reed

The March wind bends and blows a tune upon.
And yet the straw puffs up and shrieks with glee,
"Ha, ha, you see, I am a symphony."
I plod unseeing through the day,
The daily tasks, routine to the hand.
New thoughts come slowly if they come at all,
While ailing bones remind me to beware.
The future holds no joys for such as me.
The body racked with countless numbing pains
Finds sudden surcease from its many ills
And sinks to deep and final nothingness.
The mind which has no mother earth to yield,
Must roam forever, hid between the leaves
Of many books, or in the thoughts and hearts
Of later ages—living, breathing in
As formless dust, the essence of the past.

THINK OF A THE WILD GEESE FLYING

My room is lone and cold.
November's wisdom, its lesson still unlearned,
Plays merry tunes upon my window panes.
The shutters bang away in hopeless melody.
A wry sun smiles weakly through the autumn murk
While stray clouds drift silently southward
Gathering grey and bleak and ominous.

The shadows from the trees retire to sleep.
Daytime hangs tremulous on bended knee
And merriment muffles soberly into unbidden dusk.
Then momentarily a shaft of light sweeps through,
Tingling my memory with a harsher melody,
Honking a rhythm I could not fail but understand.
I think of the wild geese flying—
Southward to the Carolina marshes, the bayous and the everglades,
Southward—
In pointed swift array, wave on waning wave—
Going—going—going,
Gone—
And I am left to brood in darkness,
Tired and feeble,
Cold,
Alone.

TO THIS I CLING

I was well taught:
(When budding eyes first learned to read the law
Blazed deep in every casual stone,
Among the trees, the soil, the heart of man,
His itching fingers, his elusive brain —
And the tenuous fragrance of his mind
Freed from the accumulated rinds
And the rotted husks of many creeds,
Fetishes, fears,
And his childish animal greed.)

I have slept on beds of ashes,
Beds of stone with pillows matched,
Slept on eider-down or better,
Slept on wet remorse and shame.

And finally, the bending road comes home
And I re-view my natal hearth,
The early springs, now dried and weedy,
The saplings — heavy with the years,
The houses weary with their standing,
The neighbors resting in the fields
(With a crumbled stone to mark them.)

This — the immutable Law:
And for me, this empty codicil I leave:

Select a giant oak.
Slowly build your ladder.
Gather sticks and stones and mud,
Feathers and the blowing heather.
Climb and build
Strong and sturdy.
Climb and sing —
Then sing and rest.

MORNING STROLL

This aged pen of mine,
Steeped in the bright red ink of fire,
The black of death,
The green of clutching avarice,
The purple of confusion and of lust,
Dips queerly in the soft white liquid of the early dawn.
The paper scratches,
But still no words descend upon the waiting canvas.
No structure rises,
No trees nor shrubs
Nor the curious little figures in the human mold
To disport themselves
And whisper tales
For the mind to feast upon
And the eyes to see.

The time is not for words nor paint nor brush.
The naked canvas, like the naked day,
Is nothing
Until the paint of time shall weave its destiny
In the motley colors of the living day,
And I perhaps, shall then make poetry
From the burned-out ashes of the day-old dream.

INTERIM

I have run this course so many times.
The dust of flying hooves is in my eyes.
The din and shouting of the multitude
(Who only sit and watch)
Are ingrown in my consciousness.
The thudding flying feet
Have pounded in my brain.
The way seemed certain, the future sure.
Victory!
The screeching bands,
Ribbons,
And not the least,
The silken purse,
The bursting ego,
The universe of "I".

I have run this course so many times,
Exulted,
Floated in my magic bubble,
Around around the lengthening turf.
Now for the finish!
Spurs and whip,
The reckless dash,
Hooves.
I see them,
Hear them,
Feel them,
Before me,
After —
Choking dust.
Hooves are pounding in my marrow.
My beast and I have merged.
My hooves are pounding now.
My heart is thumping wildly.
My eyes are sightless —
Mad.

Suddenly,
The turf is gone,
The watchers silent.
I must have missed the turn.
Slowly I slacken speed,
Peer fearfully through dust-choked eyes,
Draw deeply of the first cool breath of early evening.
Panting, bewildered, I halt abruptly.

Beneath me are the fragrant grasses
I used to know so well.
The great crimson ball in the west
Is gathering up its glowing mantles
And will soon retire to sleep.
Looking eastward,
Faintly on the darkening horizon,
I see the frowzy spires of the track
Rear their ugly pinnacles
To the star-strewn evening sky.

Waiting here,
My ears have caught the melodies
Of the symphonies of night.
My eyes have seen the harmonies of swaying trees,
Of floating clouds
And a dark habitation against the moon-lit sky.

NATURE

(to the ignorant)

I am a man of many books.
The warehouse of the ages,
As bound and stored in countless volumes,
I hold my natural heritage.
I know I am the sum and total
Of the additions, subtractions,
Chemical and philosophical equations of the past,
Molded to the present,
Sheltered and protected
As a strange and exotic specimen
And curiosity.

How else,
Sitting at the rim of this peaceful valley,
And contemplating the vastness of it,
The millions of its assorted shrubberies,
The raindrops trickling from the leaves
To find their way unerringly
To the crashing rapids below,
Could I feel justified?

Before this bewildering array of teachers,
I feel unlettered,
Untutored,
In a primal kindergarten.

AND THE WALLS

Remembering the Alamo where I was born,
The boundless joy of fealty,
The desert plot my suzerain proclaimed inviolate:
My Lord commanding
I allow no dolt with heavy sledge
Belabor his virginal citadel.

Remembering the sterile soil where only cactus bloomed,
The lonely nights,
The breaking thankless toil,
And for what:-
The reaper harvesting himself instead.

The arrows fly with indifferent grace,
Like preening hawks shadowing their kill.
The tired walls strain and crack,
Disintegrate,
Rehearsing death —
And futile as any Alamo.

WHY

Why do I scribble?
Whom must I please?
Painfully dribble,
Experts appease?

Frost is so home-like,
Eastman so gay.
Sandburg the flint strikes;
All have their say.

Slowly I read them.
Swiftly I scan.
Rhyme scheme and rhythm
Seeking the man?

Looking for thunder,
Finding the clouds;
Who is to blunder
Among the white shrouds?

Life is for living:
(Poems to eat)
Pother misgiving,
My song is my feet.

THE AGE OF INNOCENCE

Age is a twin-edged benevolent sword,
Rusty on both its sides:
Beggared and brittle,
The odds seem a little
Too late,
Too little, too late.

Folly is fine
For children to dine,
For oldsters to dream
But never demean:
Far better too little —
Too late.

Time tears the weight
From the living estate,
Leaving the bones
For idling drones:
Too helpless to ponder —
Too late.

OUTWARD BOUND

A long hoarse whistle reverberates around my startled ears,
The rumbling motors roar to pulsing life,
The dark green muddy waters thrash with purposed punishment.
The dock, (I could have merely stretched my hand to touch)
Drifts slowly backward.
The houses and the wharves now come to post-card view,
Recede, diminish, then slowly pass from sight:—
And I am left alone beneath the drifting sky,
Above the heaving restless ocean floor,
Alone, but for the screaming hungry seagulls wheeling overhead,
Which my unharnessed mind tells me is Hail — farewell.

Halfway to no-where on my calendar
I stand beside the helm and steer my chartered course
By the ordered constellations crowding over me:—
And where I fail, my own disorder
Hides the gleaming manuscript.

The rising sun resets my whirling compass
And I am once again the master here,
Nudging her forward — "steady as she goes"
Land to the lea —
Larboard for dreams
And forward into spacious time,
To its hidden final resting place.

For the voyage is the joy and the life:
And for the sailor, the sea is home.

FOR TO-MORROW

Just sitting in the sun,
Dreaming,
Groping for some unfashioned word,
Some nascent thought
Or melody
To wander through my waiting mind,
Leap to my finger-tips,
To scratch on paper
And immortalize a song or poem,
Play or story
Which only dreamers have the will to find.

The scoffing sun goes home.
The chill winds rise.
The moon makes melody only for lovers,
The poet must sing in the dark.

TO-MORROW TOO

How many billions of summers have passed over this land?
How many fabulous fields have blossomed and blown?
How many winds have danced through the chattering trees?
How many rains have washed the world clean again?

This is but one field I am looking at.
I see but a single stream tiptoeing from here into eternity,
Unhurriedly.

How can I say it?
I hold at my finger-tips the froth of my civilization.
I can make an atom bomb.
I can take the hydrogen out of nature
And with it utterly destroy my fellow man.
I can take my books, my learning,
My arts, my sciences
And stack them up against my vision of to-morrow.
And what I see would make a cave-man tremble
As if his cave had been struck by fire and lightning,
Flood, famine and disease,
And the wrath of his revengeful gods.

This field, at least, is good, though simple,
Rich and faithful,
Beautiful to the mind —
And holding the certain, inexorable promise
That to-morrow too, it will be here.

IMPASSIONATA

Occasionally
When the week is done
And the shadows of these silly things I do
(To earn my bread
And salve my pride
Or hold this imbecilic station of my life)
Melt into some far perspective in my mind,
I find the time
To listen to a world of unplayed symphonies
Rising from a myriad vagrant thoughts,
Creating music, melody,
Flashes of insight,
Poetry,
Almost clear enough to grasp
And chain in books,
Wild enough for man yet unconceived,
Old enough for time to age and be uncounted
And sure enough for hope to wander in and be discovered,
Naked, clean and unashamed.

Then casually they are gone
And my room returns to me
Warmer, fresher than before
And quite desirable.

MIAMI HOLIDAY

Within my weary, pounding head,
The bells are chiming, holiday — sweet holiday:
Holiday — rest — vacation time,
Time for relaxation — time to think.
My fingers slow their nervous thumping,
My feet stop trotting, walk,
Then stop entirely.
Lord, I'm tired.
I empty out my pockets,
Keys, cards, memos,
Throw my tie away.
My other me has packed my case,
My writing gear, books —
It must be true —
I'm off.
That was twenty years ago as people live,
But by my stubborn calendar, a scant few days.

Here in the quiet of a summer's night,
With the stars so clear, so far away,
The world's immensity holds me in its sway;
And the little things we humans do from day to day
Seem smaller, pettier and unrewarding.
The shimmering ocean palpitates and breathes softly against the stone piers,
The warm waters roll against the sand,
Caress my feet, retire, and then return,
(Like a playful puppy with a new-found friend.)
I'm even pretending to fish,
So folks wont think I'm crazy;
And all the time new thoughts come sneaking in on me,
Dead gnarled trunks showing baby shoots
Hopefully, quietly stretching to the sky.
And I keep thinking:
This rented energy of my curious kind
Is only a stirring atom, forever imprisoned
In the harmless, stolid clay this shifting earth is made of.

A billion atoms before me
And a billion after
Will seek to finger this merchandise of stars
To find some reason, purpose or design,
Which answered rightly by our human race
Might add some color to our age-old claim
To be the rightful lord and master here.

So musing —
And happy for the hour to muse,
I fell asleep.

PERSPECTIVE

From where I sit,
Encased in greenish shade and colored lens,
The sky is pastel blue.
The grass is richer, greener than before
And softer to the touch.
And even I who tread so lightly on this curious sphere
Can feel the quick down-push, the audible return.
Was it youthful folly or some wider wisdom
Gleaned from the flowing river of my mind
Which placed this bench beneath an adolescent orange tree?
Wisdom, surely, to drink, to gather and enjoy
The easy fruits pouring so profusely from nature's every pore.
Wisdom, though I pay but scant attention to it,
Bids me to pause, gather up my ailing senses,
Marshal them about me as a guard
And reconnoiter this terrain for hidden foes
Bent upon annihilation of my kind.
For man is foe to nature, deadly and implacable.
And nature, while she's laughing, holds a dagger up her sleeve.

WHERE THE WILLOWS WANDER IN THE WIND

Where the brittle pavement ends
And my four-wheeled donkey squeals in anger:
Where the legend reads "Dead End —
Soft Shoulder —
Stop" —
You'll never made it:
There, with the knowledge of complete disaster,
I give my wilted steed a final cuff
And leave her be,
(The educated jack-ass she was meant to be.)

From there a trail skirts downward to the mill,
Beneath the highway,
Beyond the tracks,
Below the last farmhouse snoozing in the sun,
Over a patch of corn too wet to grow
And into the tall wild reeds bordering the stream.

The hush is now complete when I stand still
But for the wandering willows
Whispering endlessly.

PARABLE OF THE SEVEN FISHES

One was skinny and full of bone,
With tasteless meat and a heart of stone.
And one was fat, oily, and slick
And knew by rote each fishy trick.
Another by chance was strong and dull.
This herring was chicken for any gull.
One lived in a world they call a bowl
And earned his daily pinch of dole
Because of a gold-and-silver skin
Which hid from the eye the dross within.
A fifth one grew to mammoth size,
Yielding blubber for a prize.
Yet still another was a shark,
Enemy and killer in the dark
Warm reaches of the turbid sea,
Leaving no mark or tracery.
And lastly, from a humming brook,
A flashing speckled trout I took.
And we held converse, he and I,
As man to man, and eye to eye.
He then related wondrous tales
Of argosies and silver sails;
Of countless castles in the brine,
And darker secrets which are mine
Until I swam in a golden sea
And claimed as kin all fishery.

STILL WATERS

Hesitating,
Nimbly advancing,
Retreating,
Softly lapping at the innocuous sand,
Designing intricate patterns,
Erasing,
Then patiently renewing its thoughtless handiwork,
The quiet waters play and browse in the warm early spring
This fateful happy year conceived.
Here, perhaps, a man might rest and dream
And run his lazy fingers through the unresisting sand,
Search for sea shells,
And find perchance a pearl or two
The sun and sand and the romping rippling waters
Expose to care-less common view
And to my foolish pen.

The memory of these bitter years will soon erase.
For better or for ill, we hopeful humans
Cast aside the storms and winter's ice
When spring approaches
And a white sun shines through the enveloping cloud-fog
And we see faintly as in a dream
That a new day is here.

Presently I gather up the shining fragments,
Weighing the gleams in the iridescent baubles,
Sifting, turning, appraising.
Could it by merest chance be true
That the erratic course of man,
Like the waters lapping at our destined beach,
Conform to some mysterious law
Our shallow minds have failed to fathom:
That we poor poets on the shore
Build castles out of sterile sand,
Mortar from weeds,
Only to have them overwhelmed by the irresistible tides,
Swallowed up and soon forgotten,
Until another lazy poet, contemplating the desolate scene,
Builds yet another universe from an unrelated dream.

THE PARASITE

The fact remains
I did not write the poems I love the best,
Nor paint the pictures fascinating to the eye.
I have not built a single bridge
To span the deepening chasms of our time.
The food I eat was grown by other men,
The clothing, shorn from sheep I never knew.
The schools which taught me, somehow just seemed there:—
I scarcely paid a teacher anything.

Yet here I am —
Full grown — a man:
Fishing for moonbeams on a borrowed line
And hauling in the catches —
Methodically,
With arithmetic glee.
Then homeward bound I trudge my awkward way;
Unhurried through glaciered swamp and swale
To find my stubbled clearing, glowing in the sun,
Vigilant,
And eager for the lover's touch.

FOREVER THE WISHING WELL

One sorrowful day when drabness loosed my menial collar
And I was free to roam,
I wandered somewhere in the farthest space of time,
Somewhere between the lost and found.
Presently the wind sighed happily,
"This is the land of Memory."
In front of me, wraith-like in the twilight
I saw a floating city —
And all around
The laughing mountains merged with the sea —
And to one side,
No higher than the tree-tops,
The sun and moon and dinner together.

I entered softly,
Looked around and all about —
Wondering:
This silly place just couldn't be.
Memory is a swan-song forever lost.
Yet here it was —
The City-State of memory,
And in the very middle,
A white-washed wishing well.
Beyond the well old gardens glowed.
Old friends meandered through the trees.
Old sorrows unperturbed,
Played hide-and-seek with some forgotten joys.

Old jokes and frivolities played ball:—
The batters called the play.
The people cheered as I struck out —
And I cheered too.

How odd!
How odd the wishing well told ancient tales,
With never a sound or wink.
I listened,

Remembering.
Remembering the sights and sounds and smells of yesterday —
Remembering the living orchards of the mind,
The dank morass I often wandered through,
The deeds I hid,
The lies I thought
And stuffed in closets of forgetfulness.

"Wish", said the well —
"Wish — wish.
Look into my soul and wish."

I looked.
I saw the deep green well,
The whirling eddies cork-screw down into a bottomless pit —
Down — deep — terrifying —
Nothing.
"Leave a thought", said the well,
"A thought and go."
"I think," I murmured,
"I must be mad.
"I think the well is I
And I the well:
That nothing is lost in heaven or hell
But falls deep down in the wishing well."

I looked about
And all around
And I was here at home
With drabness cuddled by my side
And the morning sun, a peeping Tom.

FEAR

Out of the mouths of mewing babes,
The yapping of a frightened pup,
The whinny of a horse,
(When thunder speaks the language
The horse-mind understands)
Fear-freighted ghosts emerge
And roam unfettered through the unswept alleys of the mind.

Fear,
Foul-mouthed, degenerate,
Riding on obscure storms,
Striding with heavy feet through the gardens of our age,
Tearing reason down,
Destroying sense
And bringing to parade
Mute, unwrapped mummies,
Skeletons of old lies
Grasping and clutching at the brain
To open once again the silent sepulchres
To the fear-thrones of the past.

MISSISSIPPI

Land of the barren foothills,
Land of sterility and dust-choked fields,
Land of a poverty yielding fully of its worming fruits,
Defiantly,
As even the scrawny scrub of the vegetation
Defies the indolent tiller.
Here only the weed is fecund,
Living on God knows what,
But living.

Land of the delta region,
Low and watery,
Heavy with the soil of many ages
Sown by the rampaging Mississippi
On its down-surge to the sea.
Land of the blowing cotton,
The stagnant pools,
Malaria.

Land where the black man grows
Fecund and dumb,
Living on God knows what,
But living.

NEXT STOP SCOTTSBORO

The Chattanooga freighter
Rolls its cars around the mountain,
Pulls into Jackson county,
Puffs to the station,
Snorts and stops.
"All out for Scottsboro:
All out, all nine of you
Black little nigger lice
Swept off the freight cars,
Roped together like yearlings
Ready for the butcher.

Wait brother, hold on,
Got some white lice too,
Two skinny little female itches
Swept off the freight cars.
You know how lice breed easy in the South."
And suddenly — drama:
Black boys,
White girls,
A sleepy southern town,
Forced excitement,
"Avenge the honor of our southern maidenhood"
Grim white faces,
Guns in hand
And the judicial rope —
Dangling.

The centuries recede,
We're in the Coliseum.
In the straw pit, martyrs.
The lions enter.
The spectacle begins:
Spattering blood, crunching bones.
The lions lick their bloody chops.
Everyone is happy —
Even the Christians — in heaven.

THE TORCH BURNS LOW

> dedicated to his Excellency
> Orval E. Faubus, Governor of
> the free State of Arkansas.

The white man's back is not so broad,
Or strong and patient
As the beaten brown and yellow backs,
Low bent —
Burdened like an ox
And plodding the hopeless pathways
Beside the overflowing charities
So menially bestowed.

The white man is a whip,
A prodding spear probing an aching back,
A poet and philosopher of sorts
While contemplating his legacy of empire,
A saver of unregenerate souls:—
Not their putrid bodies, Lord,
Nor even their mummied minds, close-wrapped.
Just souls —
Black and brown and yellow souls,
Disembodied,
And flitting fearfully through eternities of time and space and
    patience
Until the white man's God may finally bestow,
(In heaven maybe, and maybe not
A long unending grassy plain
Stretching from a dark invisible star
To countless mountains of stars —
Heavens on heavens,
Ages beyond time,
Beyond reckoning,
Without his earthly human burdens —
Minus the spear —
Without philosophy —
Without pain.

What dreams these beggars dream!

CHARITY

He bends a creaking back
To pick green fagots from decaying muck,
To light a fire,
To warm a beggar
Who spurns sweet charity
And spits his spleen
On the red-eared donkey,
Carrying
Incomprehensibly
The white man's mystic burden.

Poor Brotherhood,
Only a fleeting Sunday vision —
Poor God,
Man's noblest craft
Buried in cobwebbed attics,
Dry-cleaned each Christmas and at Easter time,
Geared for sanctions or salvation
For the harried saint or sinner,
Carrying
Inanely
The white man's poorest burden.

BLEARY NEEDS A LAWYER

This is a good country.
We have a Constitution,
Bill of Rights,
Freedoms,
Jails,
Millionaires,
The not so rich,
The less than that,
Hoboes —
And the bleary scum, hibernating in the gutters.

Bleary had his "Master's" from many a tonkey bar
With a "Summa Cum Laude" every month
From our college of despair.
This was Monday morning.
He stood before the Bar and mumbled —
"Just gimme one more chance, your Honor
And I'll never get drunk no more."
At least ten lawyers heard our scholar plead his cause.
Not a noble gesture in the lot.
Bleary had no fee to pay —
Just thirty days.

SCHIZO—THE POET

Indescribably
The lamentations rise on the whimpering wind,
Perceptibly
Widening in serpentine convolutions,
Until orphaned grief,
Wrapped in his father's winding sheets,
Wails through the mutilated tunnels of the mind:
The Schizo comes,
Mummified as dust,
Floating over disordered tombstones,
Groping downward through the centuries
Into the forgotten mildewed pages of the past:
Schizo the missing link,
A poet dealing in frightened essences,
Diseased intuitions,
Emotions whose umbilical cords nurture from polluted
    streambeds of antiquity:
Schizo the wild one,
The twin,
Senseless to the now —
Lord of his bailiwick,
He, the only inhabitant —
With no one to explain
Or to command;
His eyrie,
Still undiscovered,
His poem
Unsung.

DRIFTWOOD—THIRTY THREE

Floating on the highways,
Aimless:
Friendly hoosegows hold them,
Nightly:
Stealing hitches on the freight cars:
Some die at the trestle crossings
Clinging to the brake-rods.
Feeling drivers help them make the next town.
A few may have a dime to spare.
But most, they pound the concrete, mile on mile:
No lift —
While Henry's Babbitts pass —
Alike the tin and man.
Patterned,
Moulded to shape by Great God Wealth —
System —
They're in the swim of things:
Riding swiftly on a rolling log;
The job,
An endless open stream:
Wages —
They must have room.
"Hoboes —
You no good scum,
No lift for you.
Perhaps you'll steal my watch, my car:
I'm busy anyway to-day.
Can't fool with lazy worthless bums.
Besides —
They passed a law —
No rides.
The State must know what it's about:
And I respect the law;
Except —
Oh well, not every law.
I drink,
I play the ponies on a tip:

Taxes —
The least I can.
I cheat a bit at love —
Can't be too good:
But say, a man must live to-day:"
And on and on — and —
But wait —
A mountain looms ahead:
Merger —
Must turn.
Bastards, I'm fired.
The stream flows quickly on:
No log, no job, no Ford, no home:
Driftwood on the highways —
Aimless —
System.

SONG AND LAUGHTER

Bend low, old man.
Lean heavy on your gnarled cane.
Can you hear the tulips singing in the wind?
Listen how delicately the melodies pour from the swaying petals.
Note the new-born leaves, old man,
Softly laughing at a fresh-told tale
A stranger brought while passing through.
Listen, if you can, to the daisies dancing in the meadows,
Swinging to the rhythm of the universe,
Chatting and laughing in the summer breeze.

Song weds with laughter,
And the progeny inherits the earth
In wind and water, flower and shrub,
And the sharp-nosed mountain puncturing the foot-loose clouds.
All are singing,
All dancing,
For my restless ears and watery eyes
To feast upon and be glad.

CARROUSEL

Margie and Josie and Penny McVey,
Hency and Rosie and Betty McShay,
Steven and Jimmie and Johnnie and Ray
Pretending the atom is coming today.

The atom is coming
Boom boom.

The atom is coming
Boom boom.

No Margie — no Josie
Boom boom.

No Hency — no Rosie
Boom boom.

Jimmie's the pilot and Johnnie's the crew.
Steven's the fall guy and that isn't new.
Penny is watching away in the blue
And Betty's too silly to notice the view.

The pilot's on order
Boom boom.

The world's in disorder
Boom boom.

It's only a game child
Boom boom.

It's only a game child
Doom doom.

THE FORGOTTEN MAN

I am articulate,
This once.
I am the little man
(At least I was the man)
Who was supposed to be forgotten.
I am his wife,
His Children,
His grandchildren — who will never be.
I was alive.
Until to-day,
I was poor,
Ignorant,
Overtaxed,
Underpaid,
Propagandized and presumed upon.
I tilled the soil.
I was inflated,
Deflated,
Exploited,
Robbed of my pittance;
And today,
I was shot.
It seems I didn't Heil our Fuehrer fast enough.
I stood before a wall
And thought it over.
Was I the man everyone forgot?
For one brief instant,
Looking at the brutes
Who paid me such attention,
I was glad.

TRAIL'S END

Fortune, like a rainbow in the southern sky,
Hangs tremulous on vapored sunbeams after rain.
Only the mirage is real: — for the eye to feast upon
And the mind to wonder at the supernal jokester
Making lavish sport of us dull folks on earth.

First, and almost imperceptibly, a gentle puff of wind,
A smallish cloud sailing slowly to the sun.
Then, in quick array, a mighty squadron follows,
Massing in formations for the battle soon to come.
The distant roar of heavy guns can now be heard
And overhead the flash of bursting atoms fills the air.
The wind sucks in its breath, then lets it out in giant puffs.
The trees bend grudgingly, holding on for dear life.
Finally the heavens open the assault:
Great sheets of rain come pouring through our lines,
Taking our advance positions,
Encircling us on both our flanks,
Enveloping our defenses
Until abject surrender of her imperious will has been achieved.
At last the big guns cease their pounding.
The frightening flashes come no more.
The rattle of machine guns turns to soothing patter,
And then without a warning the sun peeps through,
On a wet, bedraggled and glistening world.

I hear a final peal of laughter from above,
Look up and see a bridge of many colors span the sky.
Vainly I try to shake the clinging mud-clots from my brain
And grasp a floating spectrumed rung — to climb and climb
Until the sodden earth is distant as the shining heavens:
While I hang poised among the racing spheres
Guiding their destinies with an airy hand
Clutched tight to a glittering sunbeam from afar.

Suddenly I hear an earthless chuckle.
The bridge is gone.
My silly fist now holds some scattered raindrops.

SUNSET THROUGH A PERISCOPE

Slide into the sea,
Dear friend,
And die
In that bright and glorious way
That all light dies,
Melting into a twilight of a day well spent,
Soft and mellow
And rich with the promise of to-morrow.

Sink beneath the ruddy waves,
Old friend,
And sleep
Among the cold, black, comfortless boulders
Of the enveloping sea.

And rest,
Dear friend,
Rest, while the maggots of our destiny
Crawl and squirm
And devour in their pitiless ways
The storehouses of our yesterdays:
Until man must shrink
(Even as one of them)
And learn to kill and burn and grovel
In the filth and lust and carnage —
To extinction.

ON PARADE

Your best foot forward,
The other follows.
The pavement glitters,
The new rain spatters
On hard set faces,
Pushing the right foot forward,
Pulling the left along.

The pavement has no ending.
The rain, will it ever cease?
The slush, slush, marching onward,
Face frozen stiff as a stone
Saluting the High Command.
Your best foot forward,
The other just goes.

Your best foot forward,
The only heart you have.
Your right limb shattered,
Your left foot splattered,
The blood flows freely
Down on the hard, wet pavement,
Saluting the High Command.

A POSTHUMOUS AWARD

He fell
On a rocky slope near Tunis.
His body quivered
As it hurtled downward from the ledge
And came to rest,
Blood-spattered and muddy
In the twisted gorge between the peaks.
He was quite dead by then,
For only the Spirit could leave that open sepulchre
And climb the tortured stones to life.

I know
The rivulets will bring a fitting mantle for his grave.
I know the winds
Will play incessant symphonies over him,
And that the birds
With twig and leaf
Will build a shrine to mark the incident.

A shrine
Which mankind in its ignorance will overlook;
A shrine
From which no deep resolve will come;
A shrine for fools
Who worship silently
The unheard god of brotherhood.

ASHES ON OKINAWA

This melancholy island rising sharply
From the blue iridescent waters of the eastern Pacific
Has seemed to this unworthy teller
But yet another outpost to the prison chain
Girding our island fortress.
Here on this insignificant heap of rubble
We power-mad idiots tried our metal with your unwilling world.
And when the sun will sink beneath the shadows on the cliffs,
We too shall sink,
And all that was Japan will sink and be no more
Than a yellowed parchment scroll
In some forgotten nook where future scholars meet.

I am a soldier of Japan.
My duty called me here.
Here I have fought,
And here in the awful twilight I should have died
Amid the ruin we willed upon a misdirected universe.
It seems odd
That I should sit upon this blood-stained rock
And give you this unworthy history.
I well remember as a wide-eyed student,
I bathed in your western civilization —
Heidelberg, Vienna, Prague,
And your quaint Ohio college,
Serene and beautiful Oberlin.
Odd I turned to Jesus as my Savior.
I never saw a Christian turn the other cheek.
Japan, my honorable captors,
Is not a land of stupid barbarians,
Not a jungle for degenerate beasts,
(Though some now dwell there,)
Not a race benumbed with superstitions;
Nor do we follow blindly dictates of opinion
Which our common knowledge
Is base or evil or unworthy of our kind.
I cannot see you, yet I know you smile.
My eyes are on the altar of your might,

Burned out and hollow,
Even as my days are sered, empty and forlorn.
Japan will ask no quarter, nor any pity;
Nor will they tell you this unholy war was justified,
Or that any war is justified,
Even if it swelled our boundaries beyond our dreams,
Or those who dreamed for us while we reposed or slumbered.
Japan has wicked leaders,
Uncouth, unmoral, unscrupulous, insane,
But so have you and Britain.
It is true your thieveries are more refined,
While ours are brutal, soulless, cruel.
I take no comfort from it.

In your country you kill a dog which runs amok.
Even a dog goaded to killing,
Must be killed, buried and forgotten.
Yet the master lives —
Feeds his sickness on other dogs — on other days —
At other moments and occasions:—
And you will have another judgment to pronounce.
And still another mindless dog will die.

This I can tell you, humbly and in pain:
Deep in the shattered crevasses of their hearts
The little people of Japan have come to know
You wish them well, not evil.
Even when the heavens pour your wrath upon them,
When their temples and their gods have perished in your furnaces,
When their God-Emperor is no more,
And all that was sacred will pass and be as but a memory,
They still believe that darkness slumbers through the night
And that the rising sun will bring us light, peace—
And ultimately—
Understanding.

Farewell, my brother foe.
For me, I have lived too long and too unworthily,
Or hardly long enough.
Farewell.

ITALY

(September 8, 1943)

Where is the mourner's bench,
The stygian dress,
The hushed and vibrant silences
From the thronged assembly at the bier?
Where is the solemn face,
The pitying mien,
The poor and unremembered relatives
That blood cannot erase?
Where is the doleful will,
The joyous heirs,
The casket and the patient digger?

Where is the quickening mind,
The challenging eye,
The ear attuned to melody
And the quivering throat, to sing?
Where is that fierce joy,
The will to fight,
The stony courage of the free
And a smoking ember?

RED WINE RETURNING

The minions of the devil have ridden the winds.
In hamlet and town,
In great cities,
On barren farms
The odious winds relentlessly beckoned.
The young men regretfully left their undreamed beds,
The fulsome, waiting eager breasts
And stumbled forth to war.

That year the devil was a bartender.
Red wine flowed in the filthy gutters,
Spilled into yawning sewers,
Drained into near-by rivers,
Fertilized the bankrupt soil,
Then rose again as green-grey weeds
Covering the unsightly trash
The bartender thoughtlessly cast away.

Red wine returning,
A prayer and a tear
And a short remembering.

WIND OF THE EAST
(Overture to Peace)

Seemingly out of nowhere,
Born perhaps in the vast emptiness of the somber Pacific
Or in the jungle slime among the fetishes of decaying life,
You rose heavenward,
Hesitating—
Afraid of the intoxicating ether of your composition,
And stifling from the after-birth which held you in its bondage.

But even before the radio
Had blurted out the possibility of peace,
My ears had caught ethereal music
Played on the taut strings of a thousand swaying trees,
In the rustle of a million singing leaves,
The hushed cadences of sullen driven clouds
Thudding across the sweating storm-swept countryside
And darkening the scene with blue-gray pigments of obliteration
    and silence.

Now lightning flashes.
The violins receive the nod.
Cellos and the basses follow.
The rain-drums beat staccato.
The trumpets sound insistently
High and clear above the rest.
The kettle-drums of thunder rise from small beginning
And roll deep and terrible to its pre-ordained crescendo.
Then Comes a breath of wind, vibrant, exhilarating,
A soft caressing wind from the haze-filled East.
The players feel it,
Pause,
Lay down their monstrous instruments.
Silently they fade into the gathering past.
Only the flute still plays.
Sweet, harmonious, the music floats into the sodden atmosphere,
Filling the air with melody
Such as the dull ears of man have seldom heard
And never understood.
Blow, wind of the dawning East.
Quickly spread each casual note,
Lest the music fade—and all is lost.

THE MERRY-GO-ROUND STANDS STILL

At a thousand miles per hour, the world's a toy,
An odd shaped oval lump on a misplaced pole
Dangling in the denseless void:—
A merry-go-round for futile children
Riding their plaster ponies on a heaving stick,
Leaning fearfully into space to snatch an elusive ring
Held smilingly beyond their finger tips.

For a billion years the ponies rode the desolate trail,
Daily snorting to the sun—
Nightly, to the moon
And waving a cheery greeting to the twinkling star-brood hanging
    around.

Until—
Until suddenly the children knew Creation:
Split the plaster ponies into atoms,
The atoms into neutrons,
Shod the neutrons with hydrogen,
Harnessed them
And drove them into space.

And so—
Little Sputnik came belching,
And then his brother was spewed to the star-ways,
And others
With dogs and humans,
Laws,
The division of astral real estate,
Murder among the moons,
Statesmen mouthing nothings from the orbits,
Atoms raining everywhere:—

And the earth shuddered
And stopped.

I HAVE A COMFORTABLE GOD

I have a comfortable God,
But He hears me not in Reynosa,
Whispering in the confessional stall.
He cannot see the offerings in the cardboard box,
Nor the tallow oozing from the dying candle.
Our God is in his heaven,
Not here.
Heaven,
Is where the simplest peon is Lord in all his manor,
His house, a hacienda perched grandly on a cloud:—
And all one has to do is whistle,
Or snap a little finger—
Like so—
And a buzzing cherub snuggles up to you
To do your smallest whimsy.
But here in Reynosa,
God will come mañana.
He cannot bear the stench of unwashed bodies,
Pigsties for houses
And dung-clots covering the brains of his unremembered children,
Who neither see—nor hear—
Nor understand
That God is in his heaven—
(There to stay)
And that we, jungled and de-humaned,
Fester in the Reynosan swamp,
While the Rio-Grande mournfully gurgles past our lair
And keeps our Lord without—
Preoccupied,
Silent—
But very comfortable.

OBSERVED BY A CELESTIAL VISITOR

Alley cats snarling for the same can,
Ptomaine.
The winner dies.
Earthlings squandering their inheritance
On atoms,
Squandering the atoms
Chasing a mewing cat
Through the alleys of ancient dogmas,
Into the labyrinths of untried creeds,
Disintegrating
Cats, alleys, dogmas, creeds
And the atom itself
In the finalty of nothingness.

VALHALLA AND THE ANGELS

Thor looked out from his fortress heaven
And heard some curious noises coming from below.
Instead of the clanking anvils,
The sizzling forges
Turning the celestial steel to swords and armour,
Merry voices of his wives and children
Floated through the heavy, spear-chipped grates
And into his unaccustomed steel-shod ears.
Thor was worried.
These foolish females, wives and concubines,
And the irritating little polliwogs who tagged along,
Could drive a doodling god to drink.
The heavens had come to evil days.
No more of wars and the lusty battle cry.
No more the chariots cruising through the shielding clouds
To strike the foe before he woke.
No more the feasting and the joyful cup.
These new arrivals would not fight,
Nor play, nor drink,
Nor sortie after women when the mating season came.
They sported golden wings
And had a halo follow them.
Silly little sissy gods—
And the tall thin one they called the Christ.
Thor was angry.
He raised his creaking frame to better see the spectacle below.
The sight was salt and ashes in his misty eyes.
The women he had raised by blood and thunder,
His women,
Entertaining,
In his own courtyard,
The brazen little hussies with the silly wings.
Thor roared:
"I'll break their stupid little necks.
I'll clip their frowzy yellow wings."
Thor howled:
"My mace,

My spear,
My trusty sword.
Gird on my armour.
I go to fight this enemy—
Unto the death."
Thor wailed:
"My mace,
My spear,
My flesh and blood—
Women with wings,
Haloes."
Thor swooned.

SUNDAY IN HEAVEN

The heavens are blue,
Deep, satisfying, ethereal blue:—
Not blued-in as Monday's wash,
To come out white,
But blue until the end of space;
A kind of blue that makes the mind rejoice,
The feet to be more nimble:
It makes the houses almost decent,
Perfumes the garbage in the street:—
And even man,
Pudgy and twisted by his gleanings,
Looks almost human
When a warm sun unbuckles his hereditaments
And leaves him standing naked in the blue loincloth
Without his civilization on.

KINDERSPIEL

The gods are terrible people:
Me, in my darkest haven,
Pondering upon the scrambled world below,
And seeing the interminable herds of little men grazing fitfully,
Everlastingly around their spinning bowl,
Frenzy piled on frenzy,
Grub on grub,
Stone on ponderous stone,
Belly on belly—
Gaping jaws,
Everlastingly.

The gods are innocent people:
Me, in my brightest haven
Gazing upon the wondrous works the gods perform,
The slide-rule heavens,
The sun's unfailing time-table,
The hint of vastness—so very vast,
That contemplation clogs the keenest mind.

This little universe has gone to pot
And left me spinning in a vacuum of nebulous gyrations.
Beneath me the seething waters are pulling me down
And under—
Into the maelstrom,
Round, rudderless,
Swirling towards another shore mushroomed with light,
Folly and disintegration:—
Land we misered for—ashed and done
And sliding back to primal ooze.

This sullen universe on which I float;
This leaking bowl the gods pretend to love;
These breathless men who jostle me and steal my bread
And fall upon me with rudest hands,
These are my brothers,
Not theirs:

This flimsy earth,
All ours:
Our very own,
To work in, strengthen,
Recreate the glowing images of our finest minds,
Pull out the bung-stops, if we must
And let the wine spill down and disappear
Into the void—
But not be toyed with by some unthinking god
Killing a dullish century.

HOW IS IT?

How is it that a seed blown over the windy earth,
Until by accident it falls,
Until by some mysterious law the soil flings wide a door
And bids it welcome—
Brings food and drink,
Provides a bed, sweet music,
Company—
And when the hour is ripe,
Sends forth a flower:
That she might have her song to sing
And live her days maturely in her right,
Until a strong wind blows upon the face of the earth
In sharp, impatient summons
And gathers up her virgin seed?

How is it that a child is born with wonder in his eyes,
With itching fingers to explore his world,
With curious feet to wander in and out among the stars
And tie a string between his heaven and earth
And bring them to his finger-tips?

How is it that a child matures before his time—
Learns wisdom from an empty stomach or a rod,
Philosophy from ancient dogmas, hollow-shelled,
Politics from befuddled rattle-brains
And love—by reciprocity?

How is it that the world moves on without a rudder,
Without a captain, helmsman, or a guiding star,
Without a starboard or a leeward side,
Without a port of destination,
Without a dream,
Without a haven in a storm?

CANDLEGLOW

The sea is a wilderness of black and greys
Jungled with death,
Invisible,
Waiting:
Waiting for the shell to strain and crack
To let Death in and lead us out—
Into the void.
Inside a candle glows:
Outside,
A million candles glow,
Smothered in clouds, ambiguous and dank,
Unseen by the pigmy eyes which never learned to see;
Momentarily
Revealing eternity in a twinkle:
And unafraid, the craft rides on—
With man the argosy.

GOING DOWN

A pale sun floats out of nowhere.
It touches the blackened stacks.
Momentarily, straining my eyes,
I behold there, in genie-like gyrations,
Beautiful smoke.

I know the rest.
The blast mills are working,
The bessemer's in high.
The butt mills are grinding,
The dinkey crews are going wild.

Ore, ore,
Wonderful ore.
Dump it off the scows.
Shoot it to the dinkies.
Drop the dirty eggs
And off for more.

The white men sweat and the coal dust paints them black.
The black boys fairly glow.
Coal.
Coal for the open-hearths,
Heat and ore,
Ore and men,
Sweat and tired bodies
And steel is born.
Steel is life.
Steel is wages.
Steel is home and wife and kids,
Liquor and the sporting houses,
Guns and bullets,
Tanks and ships
And a million awful deaths.

Vulcan gloats in his bomb-proof heaven.

NEVER THE LOON

Never:
Never on this side of sanity can the mind relax:
Never the larkspur sings so clear
As the early June when the fury
Loads you down to the breaking point,
But you only bend and dream.
Never the give-and-take appears so drab,
Never the culling so obsolete
As the day the thistle blows on the lot next door
And the flash-bulb silhouettes your nakedness.
Never does reason seem so dull,
Never your work so emptying
As the flying loon you've never seen
Caresses the peak that's never been.